Be the Candle

Teadi Peter

Published by Teadi Peter, 2024.

While every precaution has been taken in the preparation of this book, the publisher assumes no responsibility for errors or omissions, or for damages resulting from the use of the information contained herein.

BE THE CANDLE

First edition. June 1, 2024.

Copyright © 2024 Teadi Peter.

ISBN: 979-8227873132

Written by Teadi Peter.

Table of Contents

Where is the Good Samaritan?

In the quiet hum of a city's heart,
Where shadows stretch as daylight departs,
Lies the tale of a soul, unadorned, unseen,
A query profound: What does kindness mean?

Where is the Good Samaritan, in this age of haste,
When life rushes by in a digital waste?
Do we see the pain behind a stranger's eyes,
Or hear the silent, unvoiced cries?

The streets are full, yet hearts seem cold,
Stories of old, often retold,
Speak of a time when aid was nigh,
When the fallen would find an ally.

But now, we pass with hurried feet,
Ignoring the destitute we meet,
Faces pressed to glowing screens,
Oblivious to what compassion means.

TEADI PETER

Where is the Good Samaritan, in a world so vast,
Where kindness seems a relic of the past?
In the alleys where shadows sleep,
In the corners where the forgotten weep?

Once, a man from Samaria came,
With no thought of glory or fame,
He saw the wounded by the road,
And lifted the heavy, unseen load.

No creed or kinship bound his deed,
Only the simple human need,
To offer help where it was sought,
A lesson in love, so dearly taught.

But now, our hearts are sealed so tight,
We shy from the suffering in our sight,
The cries for help are muted, still,
Quashed by the ever-dominant will.

Where is the Good Samaritan, in this modern plight,
Where the soul's torch seems to lose its light?
In the bustle of our crowded days,
Have we lost sight of compassion's ways?

The answer lies not far from reach,

In the lessons life still strives to teach,
In the simple acts of those unsung,
In the hearts where love is sprung.

Look to the nurse who tends with care,
The teacher who's always there,
The stranger who lends a helping hand,
The friend who helps you understand.

For the Good Samaritan lives on,
In every act of kindness drawn,
From wells of empathy deep and true,
In every me and every you.

In the shelters where hope is found,
In the laughter of children's playgrounds,
In the stranger who offers their coat,
In the lifeline of a heartfelt note.

The Good Samaritan is not a myth,
Nor confined to ancient monolith,
But breathes in deeds both great and small,
In every rise and every fall.

We are the Good Samaritans, each day,
In the choices made along our way,

In the smile given without thought,
In the battles quietly fought.

So, where is the Good Samaritan, you ask?
Hidden in each daily task,
In the courage to stand for what is right,
In the patience to soothe another's fright.

It is in the giving without a need,
In every unspoken, selfless deed,
In the moments where we choose to see,
The shared bonds of our humanity.

In the mother who wakes before the dawn,
In the artist whose work goes on and on,
In the volunteer who gives their time,
In the poet who crafts words in rhyme.

In the mentor who guides with steady hand,
In the rescuer who takes a stand,
In the doctor who mends with skill and grace,
In the lover's tender, soft embrace.

Where is the Good Samaritan? Look close,
In the hearts where empathy flows,
In the gestures that may seem so small,

Yet signify the most of all.

In the crowded streets and quiet rooms,
In the gardens where the flower blooms,
In the eyes of those who care,
You'll find the Good Samaritan there.

So let us cast our doubts aside,
And in our hearts let goodness bide,
For the Good Samaritan is near,
In every act that draws us near.

Where is the Good Samaritan? Right here,
In the love that conquers every fear,
In the hope that never dies,
In the strength of our collective ties.

For kindness is a timeless seed,
That grows in every noble deed,
And though the world may sometimes err,
The Good Samaritan is everywhere.

In the dawn of each new day,
In the light that guides our way,
In the bond we all must share,
The Good Samaritan is always there.

So be the Good Samaritan, in your life,
Amidst the noise and strife,
In the gentle touch, the loving hand,
In the grace to Care and understand.

For every time we choose to care,
The Good Samaritan is always there,
Not lost, not gone, but ever true,
In the heart of me, in the heart of you.

The Comeback

In the depths of silence, shadows lie,
Whispers of the past drift by,
A time when dreams were bright and bold,
And hearts were made of stories told.

But life, with all its twists and turns,
Its trials, lessons hard to learn,
Can dim the light, can dull the gleam,
Can shatter hope, disturb the dream.

The path once clear, now overgrown,
With doubts and fears, with seeds unknown,
The journey stalled, the spirit worn,
The warrior's heart now bruised and torn.

Yet in the darkest, deepest night,
Where stars are hidden from the sight,
There stirs a spark, a flicker, a flame,
A whisper calling out your name.

It speaks of strength, of courage deep,
Of promises your soul must keep,
Of battles fought, of victories near,
Of rising up despite the fear.

For within the heart, the fire remains,
Though hidden by the dust and stains,
A call to arms, a cry to rise,
To stand once more beneath the skies.

The comeback starts in moments small,
In whispers, thoughts, in hearts' soft call,
In choices made, in steps retaken,
In dreams revived, in faith unshaken.

The comeback is the warrior's path,
The forging flame of inner wrath,
Not against foes outside and near,
But battling doubts, transcending fear.

It's in the first step, hesitant, slow,
In the courage to let old wounds go,
In the breath drawn deep, in the stance renewed,
In the whispering dawn, in the soul's quiet brood.

It's in the morning's early rise,

In the open heart, in the clear blue skies,
In the gaze that meets the world anew,
In the strength found within, in you.

For every fall, there lies a rise,
A chance to lift, to seize the prize,
To gather strength from every scar,
To journey further, to travel far.

The comeback is the phoenix's flight,
From ashes cold to heights of light,
A tale of power, grace, and might,
A hero's journey, a soul's delight.

In fields of loss, in valleys deep,
Where shadows linger, where sorrows seep,
There grows the seed of hope's return,
A fire within, a passion burns.

Each challenge faced, each trial met,
Is not a loss, nor deep regret,
But steps along the warrior's way,
Towards a brighter, braver day.

For every tear that's shed in pain,
Becomes a river, feeds the grain,

And every heart that breaks and bends,
In healing finds, in rising mends.

The comeback is a symphony,
Of second chances, destiny,
Of dreams reborn, of hopes regained,
Of battles won, of strength maintained.

It's in the song that fills the air,
In the whispered prayer, in the deepest care,
In the hands that lift, in the eyes that see,
The boundless depth of possibility.

The comeback is the artist's brush,
Against the canvas, colors lush,
It's in the words the poet writes,
In darkest days, in sleepless nights.

It's in the athlete's final stride,
In the sailor's chart against the tide,
In the scholar's quest for truth and light,
In the warrior's vow to stand and fight.

For life will test and life will try,
To break the spirit, dim the sky,
But in the heart, the soul, the mind,

The strength to rise again, you'll find.

The comeback is the seed of dreams,
In barren lands, in flowing streams,
It's in the laughter after tears,
In the courage found despite the fears.

In every heart that's faced defeat,
There lies the strength to rise, to meet,
The dawn with hope, with vision clear,
To turn the tide, to persevere.

The comeback is a tale of grace,
Of finding strength in the hardest place,
Of seeing light in the darkest hour,
Of rising up, of claiming power.

It's not just in the grand, the great,
But in the daily, small, innate,
In every choice to move, to strive,
To cherish each moment, to feel alive.

It's in the parent's loving care,
In the friend who's always there,
In the stranger's kindness, in the child's smile,
In the enduring spirit, mile by mile.

For in the heart of every soul,
Lies the power to rise, to be whole,
To face the shadows, to stand the test,
To rise again, to be their best.

The comeback is the journey home,
Through deserts vast, through oceans foam,
It's the story of the human heart,
Of falling down, then to restart.

So rise, O soul, from darkest night,
Embrace the dawn, embrace the light,
For in each fall, there lies the chance,
To rise, to grow, to learn, to dance.

The comeback is your song to sing,
Of broken chains, of newfound wings,
It's the tale of courage, pure and true,
The story of the heart in you.

With every step, with every breath,
You move beyond the touch of death,
You claim your life, your love, your name,
In the comeback's light, you stake your claim.

So let the world see you rise,
With fire in heart, with stars in eyes,
For the comeback is the hero's call,
To rise, to stand, to conquer all.

In every heart, the comeback lies,
In every soul, the strength to rise,
So heed the call, embrace your fate,
For the comeback is never late.

The Next Chapter

The page turns slowly, crisp and white,
A new beginning comes in sight,
The ink is fresh, the canvas clear,
The next chapter is drawing near.

In the stillness of the night's embrace,
In the morning's gentle, dawning grace,
Lies the promise of a story untold,
A journey new, a heart unrolled.

From the ashes of the chapters past,
Where lessons learned and shadows cast,
There rises now a voice anew,
A song of hope, a clearer view.

The past was filled with joy and pain,
With sunshine bright and falling rain,
With moments fleeting, memories dear,
With whispered love and silent tear.

But now, the pen is in your hand,
To craft with care, to understand,
The paths to take, the dreams to chase,
The fears to face, the hearts to grace.

In every story lies the seed,
Of endless possibilities,
In every turn, in every line,
A chance to grow, a time to shine.

The next chapter is a gift of time,
A dance of fate, a rhythmic rhyme,
A call to step beyond the known,
To seek, to find, to claim your own.

In the quiet spaces of your mind,
Where thoughts untangle, where dreams unwind,
There lies the thread of tales to weave,
Of what to keep, of what to leave.

The next chapter is a beckoning light,
A call to rise, to take flight,
To soar above the doubts and fears,
To craft a future that endears.

The past is but a prologue, true,

A guide, a friend, a lens to view,
The lessons learned, the scars that heal,
The wisdom gained, the strength you feel.

For every end is a beginning,
A cycle new, a chance worth winning,
To write with heart, with soul, with care,
To breathe the truth in open air.

The next chapter is the dawn's embrace,
A journey to a sacred place,
Where dreams take flight, where hearts align,
Where you become the star that shines.

With every step, with every breath,
You move beyond the touch of death,
You claim your life, your love, your name,
In the comeback's light, you stake your claim.

So let the world see you rise,
With fire in heart, with stars in eyes,
For the comeback is the hero's call,
To rise, to stand, to conquer all.

In every heart, the next chapter lies,
In every soul, the strength to rise,

So heed the call, embrace your fate,
For the next chapter is never too late.

The ink is ready, the quill in hand,
To write the stories life demands,
Of courage found, of battles won,
Of starlit nights and rising sun.

The next chapter is the song unsung,
The melody that's just begun,
A harmony of hopes and dreams,
A symphony of flowing streams.

In every word, a truth unfolds,
In every line, a heart that holds,
The power to inspire, to move,
To change, to heal, to soothe.

For in the chapters still to come,
Lie the tales of love, of battles won,
Of journeys taken far and wide,
Of dreams that cannot be denied.

The next chapter is a canvas bare,
A story waiting in the air,
For you to paint with colors bright,

With shades of hope, with strokes of light.

It's in the love that you will give,
In the life you choose to live,
In the kindness shared, in the hand you lend,
In the promise kept, in the broken mend.

The next chapter is a quest begun,
A race that's neither lost nor won,
But traveled with a heart so pure,
With dreams that will always endure.

The past was but a stepping stone,
A path of lessons, not alone,
But now the future calls your name,
A burning torch, a glowing flame.

The next chapter is a promise made,
A future bright, a path well laid,
With dreams to chase, with goals in sight,
With courage bold, with heart alight.

So write with all the strength you hold,
With heart that's brave, with spirit bold,
For the next chapter is your own,
A story that is yet unknown.

In every dawn, in every day,
In every choice, in every way,
The next chapter is a chance to be,
The author of your own destiny.

The page awaits, the quill is near,
To write the stories you hold dear,
To craft a tale of hope and grace,
To find your truth, to take your place.

The next chapter is a beacon bright,
A call to stand, to fight the night,
To rise above, to seek, to find,
To leave the doubts and fears behind.

So let your heart the story tell,
Of dreams revived, of wishes well,
For in the next chapter, you will see,
The endless possibilities.

The past is gone, the future calls,
To build, to rise, to break the walls,
The next chapter is a journey new,
A path to walk, a world to view.

With every heartbeat, every breath,
You move beyond the touch of death,
You claim your life, your love, your name,
In the next chapter's light, you stake your claim.

So write with heart, with soul, with might,
With dreams that soar, with stars in sight,
For the next chapter is your song,
A melody that's bold and strong.

In every heart, the next chapter lies,
In every soul, the strength to rise,
So heed the call, embrace your fate,
For the next chapter is never too late.

The journey's long, the path is clear,
With every step, you'll persevere,
For in the next chapter, you will find,
The story of your heart and mind.

The ink is ready, the quill in hand,
To write the stories life demands,
Of courage found, of battles won,
Of starlit nights and rising sun.

So let the world see you rise,

With fire in heart, with stars in eyes,
For the next chapter is the hero's call,
To rise, to stand, to conquer all.

In every heart, the next chapter lies,
In every soul, the strength to rise,
So heed the call, embrace your fate,
For the next chapter is never too late.

She Was

She was the morning's first light,
A beacon shining through the night,
The dawn that breaks the darkest spell,
The whispered breeze, the chiming bell.

She was the laughter in the air,
A melody beyond compare,
The smile that lit a thousand days,
The tender touch, the gentle praise.

She was the rain on thirsty ground,
The solace lost but now found,
The heartbeat steady, sure, and true,
The quiet strength that always grew.

She was a story yet untold,
A tale of courage, brave and bold,
The pages turning, day by day,
With every word, she'd find her way.

She was a warrior, heart and soul,
Fighting battles to make her whole,
With every scar, she stood more tall,
With every fall, she'd heed the call.

She was the dreamer in the night,
A soul that soared to endless height,
With visions grand, with hopes so high,
A spirit wild, a wandering sky.

She was the whisper in the trees,
The dancing light upon the seas,
The star that shone in darkest time,
The muse that sparked the poet's rhyme.

She was the hand that reached in need,
The gentle heart that knew no greed,
With every gift, with every grace,
She brought a smile to every face.

She was the mother, sister, friend,
The one on whom you could depend,
With open arms, she'd welcome near,
With tender heart, she'd dry each tear.

She was the calm amidst the storm,

The fire that kept you warm,
The guiding star, the northern light,
The beacon shining through the night.

She was the dream that never died,
The song that time could not divide,
With every note, with every breath,
She lived in love, she conquered death.

She was the bridge across the rift,
The soothing balm, the precious gift,
The echo of a love so deep,
The promise that she'd always keep.

She was the rose amid the thorn,
The hope reborn, the new day's dawn,
The gentle rain, the cleansing tear,
The voice that chased away the fear.

She was the strength in fragile bones,
The queen that sat on humble thrones,
With grace, she walked through life's cruel maze,
With light that set the world ablaze.

She was the poet's muse, the artist's dream,
The flowing river, the endless stream,

With every stroke, with every line,
She painted worlds that would not decline.

She was the song of hearts set free,
The spirit of the wild sea,
The call to arms, the peace within,
The light that drew you back again.

She was the promise of the spring,
The first bloom and the songbirds sing,
With every step, with every dance,
She turned the mundane into romance.

She was the courage in the fight,
The justice in the wrongs made right,
With every word, with every deed,
She planted love, she sowed the seed.

She was the architect of dreams,
The builder of the endless streams,
With every plan, with every goal,
She crafted stories to make you whole.

She was the silence in the noise,
The wisdom in a world of boys,
With every glance, with every sigh,

She held the world within her eye.

She was the healer of the heart,
The mender when the world fell apart,
With every touch, with every word,
She soothed the pain, the voices heard.

She was the light in darkest night,
The guiding hand, the steadfast sight,
With every step, with every stride,
She moved the world with gentle pride.

She was the truth amidst the lies,
The sun that set the heart to rise,
With every day, with every hour,
She bloomed anew, a timeless flower.

She was the love that never failed,
The ship that through the storm, had sailed,
With every tear, with every laugh,
She marked her way, she forged her path.

She was the whisper in the wind,
The call to start, to yet begin,
With every dawn, with every dusk,
She breathed new life, she turned to trust.

She was the fire within the flame,
The constant in a changing game,
With every breath, with every beat,
She danced through life with nimble feet.

She was the hero of her tale,
The one who fought, who would not fail,
With every climb, with every fall,
She rose again, she gave her all.

She was the light, the life, the love,
The earth below, the stars above,
With every breath, with every song,
She showed the world where we belong.

She was the bridge, the path, the way,
The sunshine on a cloudy day,
With every word, with every smile,
She made the journey well worth the while.

She was the dream within the sleep,
The secrets that the heart would keep,
With every thought, with every kiss,
She brought to life a world of bliss.

She was the guardian of the light,
The warrior in the darkest night,
With every fight, with every cheer,
She made the world feel safe, feel near.

She was the poet's final verse,
The spell that lifted every curse,
With every line, with every rhyme,
She captured hearts, she stopped time.

She was the promise kept so true,
The love that knew just what to do,
With every laugh, with every tear,
She made the world feel less austere.

She was the end, she was the start,
The beating of the world's own heart,
With every dream, with every sigh,
She taught the world to reach, to fly.

She was the promise of the spring,
The hope that made the heart to sing,
With every dawn, with every dusk,
She brought to life, she taught to trust.

She was the fire that never dies,

The star that brightens darkest skies,
With every breath, with every word,
She made her mark, she always heard.

She was the light, the life, the love,
The earth below, the stars above,
With every step, with every song,
She showed the world where we belong.

She was the whisper, soft and low,
The river's flow, the first snow,
With every touch, with every glance,
She turned the world into a dance.

She was the sun on darkest day,
The guiding light, the gentle sway,
With every hope, with every dream,
She wove a life, a living seam.

She was the heart of all that's true,
The endless sky, the deepest blue,
With every breath, with every beat,
She made the world feel complete.

She was the strength in fragile bones,
The queen that sat on humble thrones,

With grace, she walked through life's cruel maze,
With light that set the world ablaze.

She was the architect of dreams,
The builder of the endless streams,
With every plan, with every goal,
She crafted stories to make you whole.

She was the love that never failed,
The ship that through the storm, had sailed,
With every tear, with every laugh,
She marked her way, she forged her path.

She was the end, she was the start,
The beating of the world's own heart,
With every dream, with every sigh,
She taught the world to reach, to fly.

She was. She is. She ever will be,
The force that sets the spirit free,
With every dawn, with every night,
She lives in us, our guiding light.

The World We Want

In the quiet moments of the night,
When dreams take flight, in soft twilight,
We envision a world so pure and bright,
A haven where wrongs are made right.

The world we want is bathed in peace,
Where conflicts fade and wars cease,
A place where love and kindness thrive,
Where every heart feels truly alive.

In this world, there's no despair,
No hunger, no pain, no burdens to bear,
Where everyone has enough to share,
And every soul feels loved and cared.

The world we want is just and fair,
Where each person's treated with equal care,
Where justice isn't just a word,
But a reality, seen and heard.

Imagine a place where nature sings,
Where rivers flow with crystal springs,
Where forests stand in majestic grace,
And every creature has its space.

The world we want is green and clean,
With skies of blue and fields of green,
Where the air we breathe is pure and sweet,
And harmony is a common beat.

In this world, we cherish the earth,
We honor its gifts, its value, its worth,
We live in tune with its rhythm and flow,
And ensure it thrives for the future to know.

The world we want is full of light,
Where ignorance flees and knowledge ignites,
Where education is a right, not a fight,
And every mind shines ever so bright.

Imagine a place where dreams come true,
Where opportunities abound for me and you,
Where creativity is nurtured and allowed to bloom,
And every talent finds its room.

The world we want celebrates diversity,

Where every culture is met with curiosity,
Where differences are embraced, not feared,
And every voice is genuinely heard.

In this world, compassion reigns,
It flows through cities, towns, and plains,
A thread that binds us heart to heart,
A world where no one feels apart.

The world we want knows no borders,
No divisions of race, no strict orders,
A global village, united and free,
Where humanity thrives in unity.

Imagine a place where health is prime,
Where care is given to all, every time,
Where diseases are met with cures and might,
And everyone lives a life of light.

The world we want is safe and sound,
Where every child can play around,
Where streets are safe, both day and night,
And every home is filled with light.

In this world, we uplift the weak,
We empower the voiceless to speak,

We stand as one, hand in hand,
And build together, across the land.

The world we want is filled with grace,
Where every soul finds its place,
Where love is more than just a word,
But the essence of our every world.

Imagine a place where hearts are free,
To love, to live, in harmony,
Where empathy is a guiding star,
And kindness takes us near and far.

The world we want is free of fear,
Where hope is strong and always near,
Where every dream is given flight,
And every day brings new delight.

In this world, art and music thrive,
They are the heartbeat, the soul alive,
They bring us joy, they make us see,
The beauty in our unity.

The world we want values the old,
Their wisdom, their stories, worth more than gold,
We cherish the young, their spirits bright,

And guide them with love, into the light.

Imagine a place where time is kind,
Where work and rest are well-aligned,
Where balance is the norm, not the quest,
And every life is truly blessed.

The world we want is built on trust,
On foundations strong, on pillars just,
Where truth is honored, lies despised,
And integrity is highly prized.

In this world, the future's clear,
It's a vision bold, without fear,
It's a promise we make to those ahead,
A legacy of love, widespread.

The world we want starts with us,
With every choice, with every trust,
With every hand that reaches out,
With every heart that conquers doubt.

Imagine a place where we all strive,
To make each other feel alive,
Where selflessness is not rare,
And generosity fills the air.

The world we want is ours to make,
With every step that we take,
With every act of love and grace,
We bring this vision into place.

In this world, we all belong,
Together we are ever strong,
With unity, we will prevail,
And write together a beautiful tale.

The world we want is not a dream,
It's a reality that we redeem,
With every action, big or small,
We create a world that's good for all.

So let us strive, let us create,
A world of love, a world so great,
For the world we want is within our hands,
A beacon shining across the lands.

Imagine a place where joy is shared,
Where every soul is deeply cared,
Where laughter rings in every street,
And happiness is complete.

The world we want is a place of joy,
For every girl and every boy,
For every man, for every woman,
A world where peace and love are human.

In this world, there's no more hate,
No prejudice, no cruel fate,
Just a charm of love and grace,
A beautiful, inclusive place.

Imagine a place where dreams are free,
Where every soul can simply be,
Where the future's bright and full of light,
And every heart is full of might.

The world we want is a symphony,
Of love, of hope, of unity,
A song that echoes through the years,
A melody that calms all fears.

In this world, we find our way,
Through night and day, come what may,
With hearts united, we stand tall,
And create a future for us all.

The world we want is within reach,

A lesson that we all must teach,
To live with love, to live with care,
And build a world beyond compare.

So let us dream, and let us do,
For the world we want is ours, it's true,
With every step, with every heart,
We bring this vision, we do our part.

In this world, we find our peace,
Our love, our joy, our sweet release,
With every hand and every voice,
We make the world a better choice.

The world we want is here, is now,
With every heart, we make the vow,
To live in love, to live in light,
And make this world a pure delight.

The Choice is Yours

The path before us splits in two,
A journey marked by what we choose,
A single step, a moment's pause,
Can lead to outcomes just or flawed.

The choice is yours, a curse or blessing,
A fate decided by your pressing,
A life shaped by the roads you take,
By every move, by every break.

The curse can come in many forms,
In whispered fears, in raging storms,
In doubts that creep into your mind,
In shadows that you leave behind.

It's in the choices made in haste,
In moments lost, in dreams laid waste,
In anger's fire, in hatred's call,
In building walls, in letting fall.

The curse is in the paths not tread,
In words unsaid, in dreams left dead,
In holding on to past regrets,
In weaving webs of broken nets.

It's in the fear that grips your heart,
That keeps you from the journey's start,
In choosing to remain in place,
Instead of joining life's embrace.

But blessings too, are yours to find,
In choices made with heart and mind,
In stepping forth with courage bold,
In crafting stories yet untold.

The blessing is in love's sweet grace,
In kindness shown, in warm embrace,
In reaching out to those in need,
In planting hope's enduring seed.

It's in the moments shared with care,
In dreams pursued, in laughter's flare,
In seeing beauty all around,
In hearing life's enchanting sound.

The blessing lies in every chance,

In every smile, in every dance,
In walking paths both new and old,
In stories written, lives retold.

The choice is yours, a gift profound,
To find the blessings all around,
To turn away from anger's snare,
To live a life beyond compare.

In every dawn, in every night,
In every shadow, every light,
The choice is there, a constant call,
To rise above, to stand, to fall.

For every curse can be transformed,
In love's embrace, in hearts that warm,
In seeing light where darkness falls,
In answering the higher calls.

The blessing is in letting go,
Of pain and fear, of sorrow's woe,
In finding strength in broken places,
In seeing hope in countless faces.

It's in forgiveness, freely given,
In living life as it's been driven,

In seeing every moment's worth,
In treasuring our time on earth.

The curse is in the heart that closes,
In bitterness that time exposes,
In seeing life through jaded eyes,
In fearing loss, in living lies.

But blessings bloom where curses fade,
In choices that with love are made,
In seeing light where shadows dwell,
In hearing life's enchanting spell.

The choice is yours, to curse or bless,
To live in fear or happiness,
To walk the path of light and grace,
Or wander in a darker place.

In every breath, in every day,
In every word we choose to say,
The choice is ours, to build or break,
To give, to take, to love, to hate.

For life is but a fleeting chance,
A moment in the cosmic dance,
A gift that's given, free to use,

A story that we get to choose.

The choice is yours, in how you live,
In what you take, in what you give,
In seeing blessings all around,
In hearing life's enchanting sound.

In every heart, the choice resides,
In every soul, the truth abides,
The power to transform our fate,
To love, to hope, to heal, to create.

The curse is in the paths we fear,
In holding back, in drawing near,
In seeing life through narrowed eyes,
In missing out on brighter skies.

But blessings bloom in open hearts,
In seeing life as it imparts,
In walking paths both new and old,
In stories written, lives retold.

The choice is yours, a gift profound,
To find the blessings all around,
To turn away from anger's snare,
To live a life beyond compare.

In every dawn, in every night,
In every shadow, every light,
The choice is there, a constant call,
To rise above, to stand, to fall.

For every curse can be transformed,
In love's embrace, in hearts that warm,
In seeing light where darkness falls,
In answering the higher calls.

The blessing is in letting go,
Of pain and fear, of sorrow's woe,
In finding strength in broken places,
In seeing hope in countless faces.

It's in forgiveness, freely given,
In living life as it's been driven,
In seeing every moment's worth,
In treasuring our time on earth.

The curse is in the heart that closes,
In bitterness that time exposes,
In seeing life through jaded eyes,
In fearing loss, in living lies.

But blessings bloom where curses fade,
In choices that with love are made,
In seeing light where shadows dwell,
In hearing life's enchanting spell.

The choice is yours, to curse or bless,
To live in fear or happiness,
To walk the path of light and grace,
Or wander in a darker place.

In every breath, in every day,
In every word we choose to say,
The choice is ours, to build or break,
To give, to take, to love, to hate.

For life is but a fleeting chance,
A moment in the cosmic dance,
A gift that's given, free to use,
A story that we get to choose.

The choice is yours, in how you live,
In what you take, in what you give,
In seeing blessings all around,
In hearing life's enchanting sound.

In every heart, the choice resides,

In every soul, the truth abides,
The power to transform our fate,
To love, to hope, to heal, to create.

For in the end, it's clear to see,
The choice is ours, eternally,
To live in light, to banish night,
To find the blessings in our sight.

So choose with heart, with mind, with soul,
To see the world as wondrous, whole,
For the choice is yours, to curse or bless,
To live in love, in Joy and happiness.

It's Possible

In the whisper of the morning breeze,
In the rustle of the autumn leaves,
In the first light of the breaking dawn,
In every heartbeat, hope is drawn.

It's possible, a dream takes flight,
A star is born, a spark ignites,
In the depths of night, in the darkest hour,
Lies the seed of an unfathomable power.

It's possible, against the odds,
With faith as deep as ancient gods,
To climb the mountains, cross the seas,
To break the chains, to set hearts free.

It's possible, to heal the scars,
To reach beyond, to touch the stars,
With every step, with every breath,
To conquer fear, to conquer death.

In the child's innocent gaze,
In the sun's warm, golden rays,
In the laughter that fills the air,
In every moment, everywhere.

It's possible, to start anew,
To paint the world in vibrant hues,
To rise again, from ashes cold,
To find the strength, to be bold.

It's possible, to make amends,
To turn lost foes into friends,
With open hearts and open minds,
To leave the past, to break the binds.

It's possible, to mend what's broken,
With loving words, softly spoken,
To build anew, with hands that care,
To lift the fallen from despair.

In the silence of a prayer,
In the love that two hearts share,
In the promise of a new tomorrow,
In the joy that follows sorrow.

It's possible, to chase the dream,

To swim against the strongest stream,
With courage firm, with spirit bright,
To reach the summit, to find the light.

It's possible, to change the course,
To find the strength, the hidden force,
Within our hearts, within our souls,
To mend, to heal, to become whole.

It's possible, to see the good,
In every heart, in every hood,
To build a world of peace and love,
To honor life, the stars above.

In the darkest night, a glimmer gleams,
In the hardest fight, a warrior dreams,
In every heart, a song unsung,
In every soul, a race yet run.

It's possible, to spread your wings,
To fly where angels fear to sing,
With faith as guide, with hope as friend,
To find your way, to reach the end.

It's possible, to find the key,
To unlock chains, to set souls free,

With every step, with every choice,
To lift your heart, to raise your voice.

It's possible, to heal the earth,
To see its beauty, its profound worth,
With every tree, with every stream,
To cherish life, to live the dream.

In the tender gaze of newborn eyes,
In the vast expanse of open skies,
In the whispering wind, the roaring sea,
In every heart, in you, in me.

It's possible, to bridge the gap,
To find the strength, to fill the gap,
With every act of love and grace,
To make the world a better place.

It's possible, to light the way,
To turn the night into day,
With every star, with every spark,
To find the path, to leave the dark.

It's possible, to dream the dream,
To walk the path, to cross the stream,
With every step, with every stride,

To find the truth, to reach inside.

It's possible, to touch the sky,
To spread your wings, to soar, to fly,
With hope as guide, with love as friend,
To find your way, to reach the end.

In the silent prayers we send,
In the love we choose to lend,
In the strength we find within,
In the battles fought, the wars we win.

It's possible, to build anew,
To rise again, to see it through,
With every heart, with every hand,
To heal the world, to make a stand.

It's possible, to see the light,
To find the courage, to fight the fight,
With every dawn, with every day,
To find the hope, to lead the way.

It's possible, to turn the tide,
To find the strength, to reach inside,
With every heart, with every soul,
To mend, to heal, to become whole.

In the tears of joy, in the laughter shared,
In the moments when we dared,
In the dreams we chose to chase,
In the love we chose to embrace.

It's possible, to find the way,
To rise above, to seize the day,
With every breath, with every sigh,
To touch the stars, to reach the sky.

It's possible, to change the world,
To see the dreams that lie unfurled,
With every hand, with every heart,
To build anew, to make a start.

It's possible, to see the good,
In every soul, in every hood,
To build a world of peace and love,
To honor life, the stars above.

In the quiet of the night,
In the first morning light,
In the whisper of the wind,
In every heart, where dreams begin.

It's possible, to dream the dream,
To walk the path, to cross the stream,
With every step, with every stride,
To find the truth, to reach inside.

It's possible, to touch the sky,
To spread your wings, to soar, to fly,
With hope as guide, with love as friend,
To find your way, to reach the end.

In the promise of a new day,
In the love that lights the way,
In the dreams that never die,
In the spirit that soars high.

It's possible, to see it through,
To find the strength, in me, in you,
With every breath, with every heart,
To build anew, to make a start.

In the laughter of a child,
In the whispers soft and mild,
In the courage of the brave,
In the lives we choose to save.

It's possible, to find the light,

To spread your wings, to take flight,
With every step, with every move,
To find the rhythm, to find the groove.

It's possible, to reach the stars,
To break the chains, to mend the scars,
With every breath, with every beat,
To find the courage, to defeat.

In the love that we receive,
In the dreams that we believe,
In the hope that we hold dear,
In the strength that conquers fear.

It's possible, to make a change,
To rearrange, to re-engage,
With every heart, with every soul,
To mend, to heal, to become whole.

In the beauty of the dawn,
In the love that carries on,
In the dreams that never die,
In the hope that reaches high.

It's possible, to see it through,
To find the strength, in me, in you,

With every breath, with every heart,
To build anew, to make a start.

It's possible, in every choice,
In every heart, in every voice,
To rise above, to find the way,
To make a better world today.

In the promise of a new day,
In the love that lights the way,
In the dreams that never die,
In the spirit that soars high.

It's possible, to see it through,
To find the strength, in me, in you,
With every breath, with every heart,
To build anew, to make a start.

In the quiet of the night,
In the first morning light,
In the whisper of the wind,
In every heart, where dreams begin.

It's possible, to dream the dream,
To walk the path, to cross the stream,
With every step, with every stride,

To find the truth, to reach inside.

It's possible, to touch the sky,
To spread your wings, to soar, to fly,
With hope as guide, with love as friend,
To find your way, to reach the end.

In the promise of a new day,
In the love that lights the way,
In the dreams that never die,
In the spirit that soars high.

It's possible, to see it through,
To find the strength, in me, in you,
With every breath, with every heart,
To build anew, to make a start.

In the laughter of a child,
In the whispers soft and mild,
In the courage of the brave,
In the lives we choose to save.

It's possible, to find the light,
To spread your wings, to take flight,
With every step, with every move,
To find the rhythm, to find the groove.

It's possible, to reach the stars,
To break the chains, to mend the scars,
With every breath, with every beat,
To find the courage, to defeat.

In the love that we receive,
In the dreams that we believe,
In the hope that we hold dear,
In the strength that conquers fear.

It's possible, to make a change,
To rearrange, to re-engage,
With every heart, with every soul,
To mend, to heal, to become whole.

In the beauty of the dawn,
In the love that carries on,
In the dreams that never die,
In the hope that reaches high.

It's possible, to see it through,
To find the strength, in me, in you,
With every breath, with every heart,
To build anew, to make a start.

In the promise of a new day,
In the love that lights the way,
In the dreams that never die,
In the spirit that soars high.

It's possible, to see it through,
To find the strength, in me, in you,
With every breath, with every heart,
To build anew, to make a start.

In the quiet of the night,
In the first morning light,
In the whisper of the wind,
In every heart, where dreams begin.

It's possible, to dream the dream,
To walk the path, to cross the stream,
With every step, with every stride,
To find the truth, to reach inside.

It's possible, to touch the sky,
To spread your wings, to soar, to fly,
With hope as guide, with love as friend,
To find
your way, to reach the end.

In the promise of a new day,
In the love that lights the way,
In the dreams that never die,
In the spirit that soars high.

It's possible, to see it through,
To find the strength, in me, in you,
With every breath, with every heart,
To build anew, to make a start.

In the laughter of a child,
In the whispers soft and mild,
In the courage of the brave,
In the lives we choose to save.

It's possible, to find the light,
To spread your wings, to take flight,
With every step, with every move,
To find the rhythm, to find the groove.

It's possible, to reach the stars,
To break the chains, to mend the scars,
With every breath, with every beat,
To find the courage, to defeat.

In the love that we receive,

In the dreams that we believe,
In the hope that we hold dear,
In the strength that conquers fear.

It's possible, to make a change,
To rearrange, to re-engage,
With every heart, with every soul,
To mend, to heal, to become whole.

In the beauty of the dawn,
In the love that carries on,
In the dreams that never die,
In the hope that reaches high.

It's possible, to see it through,
To find the strength, in me, in you,
With every breath, with every heart,
To build anew, to make a start.

In the promise of a new day,
In the love that lights the way,
In the dreams that never die,
In the spirit that soars high.

It's possible, to see it through,
To find the strength, in me, in you,

With every breath, with every heart,
To build anew, to make a start.

Africa Stolen Dreams

Oh Africa, land of sun and rain,
Of ancient songs, of joy and pain.
Your dreams once soared on wings of light,
Now stolen, lost, in endless night.

From the Nile's flow to the Sahara's sands,
Your stories etched in time's great hands.
In villages where children played,
In fields where golden crops were laid.

Your heart, so vast, so pure, so strong,
Beat rhythms of a timeless song.
In every dance, in every drum,
A legacy from which you come.

But shadows fell upon your lands,
By foreign powers, with iron hands.
They came with greed, they came with might,
To claim your dreams, to snatch your light.

They took your gold, they took your men,
They shattered peace, again and again.
With chains and guns, they tore apart,
The very soul, the beating heart.

Oh Africa, your stolen dreams,
Flow like rivers, endless streams.
In every child's tear-streaked face,
In every lost and empty place.

Your kings and queens, with crowns of gold,
Your stories, rich and brave, untold.
In whispered winds, in silent cries,
Your stolen dreams beneath the skies.

They plundered wealth, they plundered land,
Left scars so deep, they still withstand.
In every village, and every town,
The weight of chains, the lasting frown.

But oh, the spirit, strong and bright,
Cannot be quenched by darkest night.
For in your heart, the fire still burns,
In every child, the dream returns.

From Cape to Cairo, vast and free,

Your spirit soars, a mighty sea.
In fields of green, in skies of blue,
The strength of old, the hope anew.

In markets bright, in bustling streets,
In rhythms of your heart that beats.
In every song, in every dance,
The dream of freedom's second chance.

Oh Africa, with dreams once torn,
You rise anew, your hope reborn.
In hands that build, in minds that strive,
The stolen dreams, now kept alive.

Your children, strong, with eyes of fire,
Inherit dreams, their spirits higher.
With every step, with every stride,
The future bright, with dreams as guide.

In classrooms filled with eager minds,
In voices strong, in hopes unbind.
The stolen dreams now take their place,
In every heart, in every face.

Oh Africa, your dreams were taken,
But not your spirit, never shaken.

In every dawn, in morning's light,
Your future shines, your dreams take flight.

From deserts wide to mountains tall,
In every heart, in every call,
Your stolen dreams return once more,
To every child, to every shore.

In fields where golden crops now grow,
In rivers where the waters flow,
In every heart that dares to dream,
In every eye, the future gleams.

Oh Africa, with spirit grand,
With dreams that rise, with hearts that stand,
The stolen past, the future bright,
In every soul, your guiding light.

For in the night of darkest hour,
In every storm, in every shower,
Your dreams, though stolen, will revive,
In every breath, you'll stay alive.

From Cape of Good Hope to Egypt's sands,
In every heart, in every hand,
The dreams once stolen now return,

In every soul, the fires burn.

Oh Africa, your stolen dreams,
Flow back like rivers, endless streams.
In every voice, in every song,
In every right, in every wrong.

Your future bright, your spirit high,
Beneath the vast and open sky.
In every heart, in every soul,
The dream of freedom makes you whole.

So rise, oh Africa, stand tall,
In every valley, every hall.
With dreams reborn, with spirits free,
Your future bright for all to see.

In every field, in every town,
In every smile, in every frown,
The stolen dreams now find their way,
In every night, in every day.

Oh Africa, your heart so strong,
Your stolen dreams, they still belong.
In every child, in every song,
Your spirit lives, it carries on.

Oh Life

Oh life, what meaning are you made,
In light and dark, in sun and shade?
In moments brief and days so long,
In whispered words, in silent song.

You spring from birth, a tender start,
A beating pulse, a hopeful heart.
With cries of life, the journey's begun,
Beneath the stars, beneath the sun.

In early days of childhood bright,
With innocence and pure delight,
You dance with joy, you laugh, you play,
In every night, in every day.

Oh life, your meaning starts to form,
In bonds of love, in family warm.
In mother's smile, in father's care,
In every touch, in every stare.

As years go by, as time does flow,
Your meaning deepens, starts to grow.
In friendships found and lessons learned,
In passions felt, in dreams that burned.

In youth's embrace, in boldest dreams,
In hopeful eyes, in endless schemes,
You seek the truth, you chase the light,
In every wrong, in every right.

Oh life, what meaning do you hold,
In tales of love, in stories told?
In hearts that break, in tears that fall,
In moments grand, in moments small.

You teach us strength, you show us pain,
In losses felt, in endless gain.
In every storm, in every calm,
You weave your thread, you sing your psalm.

In love's embrace, in lover's kiss,
In every moment filled with bliss,
Your meaning shines, so pure, so true,
In every heart, in every view.

Oh life, your meaning lies in this,

In every joy, in every kiss.
In every bond that time does weave,
In every hope, in every leave.

You're found in dreams that never fade,
In hopes reborn, in plans well laid.
In every heart that dares to strive,
In every soul that stays alive.

In every dawn, in morning's light,
In every star that shines at night,
Your meaning glows, your truth revealed,
In every wound that time has healed.

Oh life, what meaning do you bring,
In every season, in every spring?
In autumn's gold, in winter's white,
In summer's warmth, in spring's delight.

You show us paths both wide and thin,
In every loss, in every win.
In choices made, in fates entwined,
In every search, in every find.

In battles fought and victories won,
In setting moon, in rising sun,

Your meaning shifts, it grows, it bends,
In every start, in every end.

Oh life, your meaning is profound,
In every sight, in every sound.
In music's notes, in art's pure form,
In nature's grace, in every storm.

You whisper secrets in the breeze,
In rustling leaves, in swaying trees.
In ocean's roar, in river's flow,
In mountain high, in valley low.

You show us beauty in the wild,
In every beast, in every child.
In nature's bloom, in desert's span,
In every woman, every man.

Oh life, your meaning ever clear,
In every hope, in every fear.
In every soul that dares to dream,
In every plan, in every scheme.

You guide us through the darkest night,
With promises of morning light.
In every step, in every mile,

You lead us on, you make us smile.

In acts of kindness, deeds of grace,
In every stranger's loving face,
Your meaning's found, so pure, so true,
In every heart, in every view.

Oh life, what meaning do you weave,
In every joy, in every grieve?
In every bond that time does strengthen,
In every heart that love does lengthen.

You're found in laughter, found in tears,
In every moment, through the years.
In every life that dares to be,
In every heart that's wild and free.

You're in the hope of something more,
In every dream we dare explore.
In every quest for truth and light,
In every battle, every fight.

Oh life, your meaning's in the quest,
In every heart that seeks the best.
In every mind that dares to know,
In every soul that dares to grow.

You're in the love that never ends,
In every bond that time defends.
In every smile, in every tear,
In every moment, every year.

You're in the songs we choose to sing,
In every joy that life can bring.
In every dream that lights the night,
In every soul that seeks the light.

Oh life, what meaning do you hold,
In every story, ever told?
In every heart that dares to beat,
In every challenge, every feat.

You're in the wisdom time imparts,
In every journey, every start.
In every loss, in every gain,
In every joy, in every pain.

You show us paths we never knew,
In every old, in every new.
In every hope, in every fear,
In every moment, ever near.

Oh life, your meaning's in the love,
In every heart that soars above.
In every soul that dares to dream,
In every plan, in every scheme.

You're in the bonds that time does weave,
In every hope, in every leave.
In every dawn, in morning's light,
In every star that shines at night.

You're in the laughter of a child,
In nature's grace, so free, so wild.
In every heart that dares to strive,
In every soul that stays alive.

Oh life, what meaning do you bring,
In every season, in every spring?
In autumn's gold, in winter's white,
In summer's warmth, in spring's delight.

You're in the beauty of the wild,
In every beast, in every child.
In nature's bloom, in desert's span,
In every woman, every man.

You show us paths both wide and thin,

In every loss, in every win.
In choices made, in fates entwined,
In every search, in every find.

Oh life, your meaning's in the quest,
In every heart that seeks the best.
In every mind that dares to know,
In every soul that dares to grow.

You guide us through the darkest night,
With promises of morning light.
In every step, in every mile,
You lead us on, you make us smile.

In acts of kindness, deeds of grace,
In every stranger's loving face,
Your meaning's found, so pure, so true,
In every heart, in every view.

Oh life, what meaning are you made,
In light and dark, in sun and shade?
In moments brief and days so long,
In whispered words, in silent song.

You teach us strength, you show us pain,
In losses felt, in endless gain.

In every storm, in every calm,
You weave your thread, you sing your psalm.

In every dawn, in morning's light,
In every star that shines at night,
Your meaning glows, your truth revealed,
In every wound that time has healed.

You're in the love that never ends,
In every bond that time defends.
In every smile, in every tear,
In every moment, every year.

Oh life, your meaning lies in this,
In every joy, in every kiss.
In every bond that time does weave,
In every hope, in every leave.

You're in the hope of something more,
In every dream we dare explore.
In every quest for truth and light,
In every battle, every fight.

You're found in laughter, found in tears,
In every moment, through the years.
In every life that dares to be,

In every heart that's wild and free.

Oh life, your meaning's ever clear,
In every hope, in every fear.
In every soul that dares to dream,
In every plan, in every scheme.

You guide us through the darkest night,
With promises of morning light.
In every step, in every mile,
You lead us on, you make us smile.

In acts of kindness, deeds of grace,
In every stranger's loving face,
Your meaning's found, so pure, so true,
In every heart, in every view.

Oh life, what meaning do you weave,
In every joy, in every grieve?
In every bond that time does strengthen,
In every heart that love does lengthen.

You're found in dreams that never fade,
In hopes reborn, in plans well laid.
In every heart that dares to strive,
In every soul that stays alive.

You're in the beauty of the wild,
In every beast, in every child.
In nature's bloom, in desert's span,
In every woman, every man.

Oh life, what meaning do you hold,
In tales of love, in stories told?
In hearts that break, in tears that fall,
In moments grand, in moments small.

You're in the wisdom time imparts,
In every journey, every start.
In every loss, in every gain,
In every joy, in every pain.

Oh life, your meaning is profound,
In every sight, in every sound.
In music's notes, in art's pure form,
In nature's grace, in every storm.

You whisper secrets in the breeze,
In rustling leaves, in swaying trees.
In ocean's roar, in river's flow,
In mountain high, in valley low.

You show us beauty in the wild,
In every beast, in every child.
In nature's bloom, in desert's span,
In every woman, every man.

Oh life, your meaning lies in this,
In every joy, in every kiss.
In every bond that time does weave,
In every hope, in every leave.

You're in the dreams that dare to soar,
In hearts that seek, in minds that explore.
In every soul that dares to be,
In every heart that's wild and free.

Dreams of My Child

My child, your dreams are painted bright,
In colors bold, in shades of light.
They soar on wings of pure delight,
In realms of joy, in skies of might.

In your dreams, my sweet, you're free,
To be anything you wish to be.
A dragon tamer, brave and bold,
Or a guardian of stories untold.

You dream of castles in the air,
Of worlds beyond, without a care.
In fields where unicorns do play,
And night is but the end of day.

Your dreams are filled with laughter's sound,
Where happiness and love abound.
You dream of friends both near and far,
And journeys taken to the stars.

In your dreams, the ocean's wide,
A place where magic worlds collide.
You swim with dolphins, dive so deep,
In waters calm, in dreams you keep.

You dream of forests, lush and green,
Where fairies dance, where elves are seen.
You wander paths where dreams are made,
In canopies of light and shade.

My child, your dreams are wondrous things,
With dragons' fires and angels' wings.
In lands where time does not exist,
And every thought becomes a mist.

You dream of mountains tall and grand,
Of distant, far-off, mystic lands.
You climb to peaks, where eagles fly,
And touch the clouds that kiss the sky.

In dreams, you're strong, a hero true,
With courage bright, with heart anew.
You fight the battles, win the wars,
With valor that the world adores.

You dream of peace, a gentle land,

Where hearts are kind and join in hand.
A world where every soul is free,
Where love and light are meant to be.

In dreams, you sail the skies above,
On wings of hope, on wings of love.
You chart a course through endless night,
With stars as guides, with dreams in sight.

You dream of cities, vast and grand,
Where rivers flow through every land.
A place where wisdom lights the way,
And night is but a shade of day.

Your dreams, my child, are tales to tell,
Of realms where wonders ever dwell.
In stories spun from light and grace,
In every thought, in every space.

You dream of futures bright and clear,
Of tomorrows without fear.
A world where dreams do all come true,
Where skies are wide, where seas are blue.

In dreams, you're always reaching high,
To touch the moon, to kiss the sky.

With eyes alight, with heart so pure,
You see the world, you know for sure.

You dream of friendships deep and strong,
Of bonds that last a lifetime long.
With every heart you choose to bind,
You leave a trail of love behind.

In dreams, you find the answers clear,
To every doubt, to every fear.
You know the path, you see the light,
In every wrong, you find the right.

You dream of wisdom, old and wise,
In ancient books, in knowing eyes.
You seek the truths of ages past,
And find the lessons meant to last.

Your dreams, my child, are rivers wide,
That flow through time, that never hide.
They carry you to places new,
To lands of gold, to skies of blue.

You dream of gardens, full of bloom,
Of fragrant flowers, of sweet perfume.
In every petal, in every leaf,

You find a world beyond belief.

In dreams, you build with hands so sure,
A future bright, a world so pure.
With every brick, with every stone,
You craft a place that's all your own.

You dream of love, a beacon bright,
That guides you through the darkest night.
With every beat, with every breath,
You conquer life, you conquer death.

In dreams, you're wise beyond your years,
You soothe the world, you calm the fears.
With gentle hands, with loving heart,
You mend the world, you play your part.

You dream of stars, of cosmic light,
Of galaxies that fill the night.
You reach for them with open mind,
And find the truths that others find.

Your dreams, my child, are pure and true,
A mirror of the best in you.
They shine with light, they soar with grace,
In every heart, in every space.

In dreams, you find the paths to take,
To build, to grow, to mend, to make.
You see the world as it can be,
With eyes of love, with heart so free.

You dream of futures wide and grand,
Of peace that spreads through every land.
A world where every soul is kind,
Where love and light are intertwined.

In dreams, you dance on clouds above,
With feet so light, with heart of love.
You twirl through life with pure delight,
In every day, in every night.

Your dreams, my child, are gifts so rare,
They show a world beyond compare.
A place where every heart can see,
The beauty of what's meant to be.

In dreams, you write with pen so bold,
The stories of a life untold.
With every word, with every line,
You shape the world, you make it shine.

You dream of courage, true and bright,
Of standing tall, of doing right.
In every act, in every deed,
You plant the seeds of love's great creed.

In dreams, you find the strength to be,
The best that you can ever be.
With heart of gold, with soul of light,
You blaze a path through darkest night.

You dream of journeys far and wide,
Of adventures taken side by side.
With every step, with every mile,
You find the joy, you find

Let Your Reason Get Your Back Up

In times of doubt and swirling storm,
When shadows creep and fears are born,
Stand tall and let your reason rise,
With clarity to clear the skies.

When whispers fill the midnight air,
With doubts that seem beyond repair,
Let logic be your guiding light,
To turn the dark to morning bright.

Let your reason get your back up,
In every challenge, every cup,
Of sorrow deep or joy so pure,
With reason's strength, you can endure.

In moments when emotions flare,
And passions rage beyond compare,
Let reason be your calming sea,
To sail you through with certainty.

For reason's path is steady, sure,
A beacon bright, a cure-all cure.
In chaos wild, in restless mind,
It's reason's voice that helps you find.

When anger's flame begins to rise,
And blinds you to the clearer skies,
Let reason cool the heated heart,
And guide you to a better start.

Let your reason get your back up,
In every storm, in every hiccup,
With steadfast mind and measured thought,
With reason's light, no battles fought.

When love is tested, friendships strained,
And every word feels like a chain,
Let reason speak with gentle tone,
To mend the ties that are your own.

In every quarrel, every fight,
When wrong seems right and right seems slight,
Let reason be the bridge you build,
To cross the gaps where hearts are filled.

Let your reason get your back up,

In moments fierce, in times corrupt,
With wisdom clear and vision keen,
With reason's grace, all is serene.

When dreams are dashed and hopes are frail,
And every effort seems to fail,
Let reason guide your weary soul,
To find the path that makes you whole.

For reason sees beyond the now,
To future's light, to future's vow.
In every setback, every fall,
It's reason's hand that lifts us all.

Let your reason get your back up,
In every twist, in every setup,
With calm resolve and steady hand,
With reason's touch, you take your stand.

When life's demands are pressing hard,
And every turn seems fraught, unmarred,
Let reason be your guiding star,
To show you truly who you are.

In choices tough, decisions great,
When fate does knock upon your gate,

Let reason's voice be loud and clear,
To steer you through with heart sincere.

Let your reason get your back up,
In times of joy, in times of hiccup,
With balanced thought and careful view,
With reason's light, you find what's true.

When seeking truth in tangled lies,
In every mask, in each disguise,
Let reason be your keenest sight,
To pierce the dark, to find the right.

For reason's truth is pure and clean,
In every shade, in every scene.
It cuts through fog, it breaks the chain,
To free your mind from every strain.

Let your reason get your back up,
In every rise, in every slip-up,
With steady gaze and thoughtful mind,
With reason's light, your way you'll find.

In every goal you strive to reach,
In every lesson life does teach,
Let reason be your closest friend,

To guide you through to journey's end.

When doubts arise and fears take hold,
And every step feels dark and cold,
Let reason's warmth be by your side,
To light the path, to be your guide.

Let your reason get your back up,
In every test, in every buildup,
With patience deep and insight bright,
With reason's touch, you'll find your might.

For reason is the steady hand,
In raging seas, on shifting sand.
It anchors you in truth and grace,
It shows you how to find your place.

When challenges seem all too vast,
And every effort feels surpassed,
Let reason be the strength you draw,
To find the path, to stand in awe.

Let your reason get your back up,
In every doubt, in every setup,
With faith in thought, with trust in mind,
With reason's light, your truth you'll find.

In every dream you dare to chase,
In every goal, in every race,
Let reason be the guiding force,
To keep you true, to set your course.

When failure looms and hopes seem thin,
And every loss feels like a sin,
Let reason lift your spirit high,
To see the truth beyond the lie.

Let your reason get your back up,
In every fall, in every hiccup,
With calm resolve and thoughtful grace,
With reason's light, you'll find your place.

For reason's touch is steady, strong,
It helps you right where you belong.
In every trial, in every test,
It's reason's voice that brings the best.

When anger's fire begins to burn,
And thoughts of peace are hard to earn,
Let reason cool your heated mind,
To find the path, to be kind.

Let your reason get your back up,
In every rage, in every setup,
With patience deep and vision clear,
With reason's touch, you conquer fear.

In every love that blooms and grows,
In every heart that overflows,
Let reason be the steady stream,
To guide you through each waking dream.

When passions rise and blind the eye,
And every word feels like a lie,
Let reason's voice be calm and true,
To find the love that's deep in you.

Let your reason get your back up,
In every love, in every hiccup,
With balanced thought and gentle hand,
With reason's light, you'll understand.

In every joy and every pain,
In every loss and every gain,
Let reason be your closest friend,
To guide you through to journey's end.

When life's demands are pressing hard,

And every step seems all but marred,
Let reason be your guiding star,
To show you truly who you are.

Let your reason get your back up,
In every task, in every setup,
With faith in thought and trust in mind,
With reason's light, your way you'll find.

In every choice you make each day,
In every word you choose to say,
Let reason be the guiding force,
To keep you true, to set your course.

When doubts arise and fears take hold,
And every step feels dark and cold,
Let reason's warmth be by your side,
To light the path, to be your guide.

Let your reason get your back up,
In every doubt, in every hiccup,
With patience deep and insight bright,
With reason's touch, you'll find your might.

For reason is the steady hand,
In raging seas, on shifting sand.

It anchors you in truth and grace,
It shows you how to find your place.

When challenges seem all too vast,
And every effort feels surpassed,
Let reason be the strength you draw,
To find the path, to stand in awe.

Let your reason get your back up,
In every test, in every setup,
With faith in thought, with trust in mind,
With reason's light, your truth you'll find.

In every dream you dare to chase,
In every goal, in every race,
Let reason be the guiding force,
To keep you true, to set your course.

When failure looms and hopes seem thin,
And every loss feels like a sin,
Let reason lift your spirit high,
To see the truth beyond the lie.

Let your reason get your back up,
In every fall, in every hiccup,
With calm resolve and thoughtful grace,

With reason's light, you'll find your place.

For reason's touch is steady, strong,
It helps you right where you belong.
In every trial, in every test,
It's reason's voice that brings the best.

When anger's fire begins to burn,
And thoughts of peace are hard to earn,
Let reason cool your heated mind,
To find the path, to be kind.

Let your reason get your back up,
In every rage, in every setup,
With patience deep and vision clear,
With reason's touch, you conquer fear.

In every love that blooms and grows,
In every heart that overflows,
Let reason be the steady stream,
To guide you through each waking dream.

When passions rise and blind the eye,
And every word feels like a lie,
Let reason's voice be calm and true,
To find the love that's deep in you.

Let your reason get your back up,
In every love, in every hiccup,
With balanced thought and gentle hand,
With reason's light, you'll understand.

In every joy and every pain,
In every loss and every gain,
Let reason be your closest friend,
To guide you through to journey's end.

When life's demands are pressing hard,
And every step seems all but marred,
Let reason be your guiding star,
To show you truly who you are.

Let your reason get your back up,
In every task, in every setup,
With faith in thought and trust in mind,
With reason's light, your way you'll find.

For reason is the steady hand,
In raging seas, on shifting sand.
It anchors you in truth and grace,
It shows you how to find your place.

When challenges seem all too vast,
And every effort feels surpassed,
Let reason be the strength you draw,
To find the path, to stand in awe.

Let your reason get your back up,
In every test, in every setup,
With faith in thought, with trust in mind,
With reason's light, your truth you'll find.

For reason's voice is calm and clear,
It lifts you up, it draws you near.
In every challenge, every fight,
It's reason's touch that brings the light.

Oh My Destiny

In the first light of dawn, as the world wakes anew,
I search for a path, for a glimpse of a clue.
Through the whispering winds, through the morning dew,
I ask once more, "My destiny, where are you?"

In the hustle of the day, amidst the endless chase,
In the crowd's busy hum, in each hurried pace,
In the laughter and tears, in the old and the new,
I wonder aloud, "My destiny, where are you?"

In the changing seasons, in the autumn leaves' flight,
In the cold grip of winter, in spring's gentle light,
In summer's warm embrace, in the skies so blue,
I seek your presence, "My destiny, where are you?"

In the pages of books, in stories told,
In the wisdom of the young, in the courage of the old,
In lessons learned, in the trials we go through,
I ponder deeply, "My destiny, where are you?"

In the eyes of a stranger, in a friend's loving gaze,
In moments of triumph, in times of malaise,
In the joys of the present, in memories that strew,
I whisper softly, "My destiny, where are you?"

In the roads that I travel, in the choices I make,
In the dreams that I harbor, in the chances I take,
In the peaks and the valleys, in skies gray and blue,
I search and I question, "My destiny, where are you?"

In the stillness of prayer, in the solitude of night,
In the glimmer of hope, in the faintest light,
In the echoes of dreams, in the silence that's true,
I seek your guidance, "My destiny, where are you?"

In the touch of a hand, in the warmth of embrace,
In the moments of love, in the challenges I face,
In the rise after fall, in the struggle through,
I yearn to find you, "My destiny, where are you?"

In the twilight's soft glow, in the dawn's first rays,
In the midst of the storm, in the calm after days,
In the whispers of dreams, in the echoes of truth,
I call out to you, "My destiny, where are you?"

In the mirror's reflection, in the soul-searching gaze,

In the quest for purpose, in life's intricate maze,
In the depth of my being, in the dreams I pursue,
I cry with longing, "My destiny, where are you?"

In the steps that I take, in the paths that unfold,
In the stories I write, in the tales yet untold,
In the fears that I face, in the courage to renew,
I question with hope, "My destiny, where are you?"

In the hands that I hold, in the hearts that I touch,
In the connections I make, in moments that clutch,
In the weave of life's fabric, in the journey's hue,
I seek with fervor, "My destiny, where are you?"

In the silent prayers whispered, in the hopes of the night,
In the love that I give, in the wrongs I make right,
In the strength to move forward, in the dreams I construe,
I ask again, "My destiny, where are you?"

In the courage to dream, in the will to aspire,
In the spark of the heart, in the soul's quiet fire,
In the essence of being, in the life's vivid view,
I call to the heavens, "My destiny, where are you?"

In the lessons of living, in the wisdom I gain,
In the joys and the sorrows, in pleasure and pain,

In the search for meaning, in the life I ensue,
I ponder deeply, "My destiny, where are you?"

In the laughter of children, in the wisdom of age,
In stories of life, inscribed on each page,
In moments of stillness, in chaos too,
I seek for the answer, "My destiny, where are you?"

In mountains so high, in valleys so deep,
In dreams that I nurture, in promises I keep,
In the journey of life, in paths that I choose,
I ask with longing, "My destiny, where are you?"

In stars in the sky, in moon's gentle light,
In beauty of day, in mystery of night,
In calm of the sea, in storm's fierce brew,
I seek your guidance, "My destiny, where are you?"

In silent moments of prayer, in answers not found,
In peace of the moment, in earth's sacred ground,
In stillness of time, in life's grand view,
I whisper softly, "My destiny, where are you?"

In courage to dream, in power to strive,
In will to survive, in reason to thrive,
In essence of being, in life I pursue,

I call to the heavens, "My destiny, where are you?"

In laughter shared, in tears that fall,
In love that binds, in stories that call,
In journey of life, in paths I ensue,
I seek with fervor, "My destiny, where are you?"

In echo of the past, in promise of new,
In dreams that I dream, in things that I do,
In whisper of the wind, in song of the blue,
I ask with hope eternal, "My destiny, where are you?"

In moments of doubt, in moments of grace,
In search for my path, in truths I embrace,
In journey of life, in things I pursue,
I seek and wonder, "My destiny, where are you?"

In courage to rise, in will to prevail,
In moments of triumph, in times that I fail,
In whispers of hope, in dreams I pursue,
I cry out with longing, "My destiny, where are you?"

In beauty of life, in essence of being,
In dreams that I hold, in things I'm seeing,
In search for meaning, in paths I construe,
I seek with a fervent heart, "My destiny, where are you?"

TEADI PETER

In silence of night, in promise of dawn,
In battles I fight, in victories won,
In dreams that I dream, in life that I view,
I ask with an open heart, "My destiny, where are you?"

In laughter of friends, in love that I share,
In moments of joy, in times that I care,
In journey of life, in paths that I choose,
I seek and question, "My destiny, where are you?"

In whispers of dreams, in echo of truth,
In courage to strive, in moments of youth,
In love that I give, in life that I view,
I seek with determination, "My destiny, where are you?"

In moments of stillness, in times of despair,
In strength to move on, in love that I bear,
In dreams that I chase, in visions I view,
I cry out with passion, "My destiny, where are you?"

In beauty of life, in essence of being,
In dreams that I hold, in things I'm seeing,
In search for meaning, in paths I construe,
I seek with a fervent heart, "My destiny, where are you?"

In echoes of the past, in promise of new,
In dreams that I dream, in things that I do,
In whisper of the wind, in song of the blue,
I ask with hope eternal, "My destiny, where are you?"

In moments of doubt, in moments of grace,
In search for my path, in truths I embrace,
In journey of life, in things I pursue,
I seek and wonder, "My destiny, where are you?"

In courage to rise, in will to prevail,
In moments of triumph, in times that I fail,
In whispers of hope, in dreams I pursue,
I cry out with longing, "My destiny, where are you?"

In beauty of life, in essence of being,
In dreams that I hold, in things I'm seeing,
In search for meaning, in paths I construe,
I seek with a fervent heart, "My destiny, where are you?"

In silence of night, in promise of dawn,
In battles I fight, in victories won,
In dreams that I dream, in life that I view,
I ask with an open heart, "My destiny, where are you?"

In laughter of friends, in love that I share,

In moments of joy, in times that I care,
In journey of life, in paths that I choose,
I seek and question, "My destiny, where are you?"

I don't get it

I really don't get it, this maze of life's plan,
Each turn, a new riddle, where answers just ran.
The whispers of why in the silence of night,
Leave questions unanswered, though I search with all might.

I really don't get it, the paths we must take,
The forks in the road, the decisions we make.
Are we but wanderers in fate's unseen hand,
Or authors of stories we barely understand?

I really don't get it, the ebb and the flow,
The highs and the lows, the things we don't know.
The laughter that fades into tears all too fast,
The future that's shadowed by echoes of past.

I really don't get it, the reason we're here,
The dreams that we chase, the moments we fear.
Is there a meaning in the chaos we see,
Or are we just drifting, like leaves on a tree?

I really don't get it, but perhaps that's okay,
For mystery lingers in the light of each day.
In questions unanswered, in wonders unmet,
Life's beauty is found in the things we don't get.

The Great Life Siege

We march through the days, in armor of hope,
Against unseen foes, with which we must cope.
The nights whisper tales of battles hard-fought,
Of dreams nearly shattered, and lessons unsought.

The great life siege begins with our birth,
When we're thrust into conflict, to prove our worth.
From the cradle we climb, to the unknown ahead,
Facing struggles that wait, like secrets unsaid.

We fight against time, an unyielding foe,
With each passing hour, our courage must grow.
The seconds, relentless, keep ticking away,
As we strive to find meaning in each fleeting day.

In the great life siege, we encounter our fears,
The phantoms that rise from the depths of our tears.
They challenge our spirit, and test our resolve,
As we seek to endure, and to somehow evolve.

There are battles with doubt, that cloud our sight,
Casting shadows on dreams that once burned so bright.
In the trenches of worry, we toil and we strive,
Seeking solace and peace, just to feel alive.

In the heat of the siege, we struggle for air,
Gasping for moments of calm, amidst despair.
We wrestle with sorrow, with grief and with pain,
In the hopes that our efforts will not be in vain.

The great life siege is waged in our hearts,
With every joy found, and each loss that departs.
It's a war of endurance, of patience and grace,
As we navigate trials in this temporal space.

Allies we find, in the midst of our plight,
Those who stand by our side, through the darkest of night.
Their voices a balm, their presence a shield,
In the relentless assault, where strength is revealed.

We build up our courage, in layers and layers,
Drawing strength from our hopes, from our dreams, from our prayers.
In the great life siege, we learn to stand tall,
To fight for our purpose, in spite of it all.

There are victories sweet, though small they may seem,

In each moment of love, in each realized dream.
We savor the triumphs, the battles well-won,
The scars that remind us of what we've become.

The great life siege is relentless, yet kind,
For in struggle, we find the growth of the mind.
In the crucible's heat, our souls are refined,
Emerging more vibrant, more pure, more aligned.

We fight on with valor, with spirit, with might,
Against the encroaching and infinite night.
With each step we take, in this siege of the soul,
We inch ever closer to a unified whole.

The great life siege, though daunting and vast,
Is a journey of moments, not meant to outlast.
For in every heart, a warrior resides,
Forging a path through life's turbulent tides.

So we march ever forward, through tempest and calm,
With hope as our anthem, with love as our psalm.
In the great life siege, our stories are told,
Of battles that shaped us, and hearts that turned bold.

And when the last trumpet of struggle does sound,
When the echoes of conflict no longer abound,

We'll stand in the silence, where peace gently frees,
Having conquered the trials of the great life siege.

The Freedom We Want

The freedom we seek is more than just words,
It's the essence of life, where passion unfurls.
It's the right to be heard, the right to be seen,
To live without fear, to chase every dream.

It's the freedom to love, without bounds or restraints,
To embrace every color, every shade, every taint.
To celebrate differences, to honor each voice,
To stand tall together, and make our own choice.

The freedom we want is not bound by chains,
Nor shackled by fear, nor dulled by disdain.
It's the right to be different, to break from the norm,
To dance to our rhythm, in the eye of the storm.

It's the freedom to speak, without fear of reprisal,
To challenge the status quo, to ignite the revival.
To raise up our voices, in chorus and song,
To right the world's injustices, where they've been wronged.

The freedom we seek is a beacon of light,
Guiding us forward, through the darkest of night.
It's the hope of tomorrow, the promise of dawn,
A vision of unity, where all can belong.

It's the freedom to wander, to roam far and wide,
To explore every corner, with nothing to hide.
To chart our own course, on the sea of our fate,
To navigate boldly, through love and through hate.

It's the freedom to dream, with eyes open wide,
To imagine the impossible, to reach for the sky.
To believe in the magic, that lies deep within,
To create our own destiny, where we've never been.

The freedom we want is a flame burning bright,
A beacon of hope, in the depths of the night.
It's the right to be human, imperfect and flawed,
To learn from our failures, to rise with each nod.

It's the freedom to worship, in temples of choice,
To honor our faith, with one unified voice.
To find solace in prayer, in silence, in song,
To embrace our beliefs, where we all belong.

The freedom we seek is a gift to us all,

To stand tall together, and answer the call.
To build a new world, where justice prevails,
Where love knows no borders, and kindness prevails.

It's the freedom to live, without fear or restraint,
To cherish each moment, without complaint.
To bask in the beauty, of life's fleeting dance,
To embrace every chance, with open hands.

So let us stand together, hand in hand,
And fight for the freedom, that's at our command.
For in unity lies strength, in diversity, grace,
And together, we'll create a brighter place.

The freedom we want is within our reach,
If only we're willing, to practice what we preach.
So let's stand as one, in the face of the fight,
And claim our freedom, with all of our might.

My Problem, You Are

You linger in the shadows, unseen but felt,
A constant presence, where chaos dwelt.
You are the puzzle I cannot solve,
The riddle that revolves and evolves.

You are the weight upon my chest,
The voice that never lets me rest.
You cloud my vision, obscure my sight,
A never-ending, relentless plight.

You are the storm that rages within,
The battle I struggle, but cannot win.
You haunt my dreams, disrupt my peace,
A gnawing ache that will not cease.

You are the doubt that gnaws at my soul,
The fear that keeps me from feeling whole.
You whisper lies, you sow mistrust,
A poison that corrodes and rusts.

You are the shadow that dims my light,
The darkness that shrouds my every fight.
You hold me back, you chain me down,
A weight that pulls me to the ground.

You are the echo of past mistakes,
The regret that my heart cannot shake.
You haunt my memories, you cloud my mind,
A ghost of failures left behind.

You are the worry that eats away,
The anxiety that colors my day.
You steal my joy, you dampen my cheer,
A constant presence, always near.

But in the depths of despair, a glimmer gleams,
A ray of hope, a light that beams.
For though you may haunt me, you cannot win,
I'll rise above you, I'll break free from within.

For my problem, you are, but not my defeat,
I'll conquer you, I'll rise to my feet.
With courage and strength, I'll face you head-on,
And in victory, my true self will dawn.

I'll silence your whispers, dispel your lies,

I'll banish the doubt that clouds my skies.
I'll embrace my flaws, I'll learn to forgive,
And in the journey, I'll truly live.

For you may be my problem, but I hold the key,
To unlock the shackles and set myself free.
With determination and faith, I'll overcome,
And in the end, my battles will be won.

So linger in the shadows, if you must,
But know that in me, you'll find no trust.
For I am more than my problems, my fears,
I am the strength that perseveres.

And though you may try to hold me back,
I'll break through the barriers, I'll stay on track.
For my problem, you are, but I am the solution,
And with resilience and resolve, I'll find absolution.

Useless Not Am I

Useless not am I, for I have purpose untold,
A destiny waiting, for me to behold.
I may stumble and falter, along the way,
But I'll rise from the ashes, stronger each day.

I may not fit the mold, society demands,
But I refuse to be shackled, by its commands.
For my worth is not measured, by titles or gold,
But by the love in my heart, and the stories I've told.

Useless not am I, for I have a voice,
To speak up for justice, to make the right choice.
I'll stand up for the marginalized, the oppressed,
For in their struggles, I see my own quest.

I may not have the answers, to life's mysteries deep,
But I'll search for the truth, even as I weep.
For in the journey of learning, I find my strength,
A resilience that carries me, to any length.

Useless not am I, for I have the power,
To uplift the broken, in their darkest hour.
I'll lend a hand to those in need,
For in kindness and compassion, I plant a seed.

I may not have the skills, of a masterful hand,
But I'll create beauty, in the way I understand.
For art is subjective, in its many forms,
And in expression, my soul transforms.

Useless not am I, for I have a heart,
To love and to cherish, to play my part.
I'll spread joy and laughter, wherever I go,
For in connection and friendship, my spirit will grow.

I may not be perfect, in all that I do,
But I'll strive for improvement, to see things anew.
For growth lies in failure, as much as success,
And in resilience and perseverance, I find progress.

Useless not am I, for I am alive,
With dreams and desires, ready to thrive.
I'll seize each moment, with passion and zest,
For in living fully, I am at my best.

So though doubts may linger, and fears may arise,

I'll hold onto hope, with unwavering eyes.
For useless not am I, in the grand scheme of things,
But a warrior of light, with purpose that sings.

A Chance, Give Me

Give me a chance to spread my wings,
To soar above the clouds, where freedom sings.
To explore uncharted lands, and seas,
To embrace the adventure, wherever it leads.

Give me a chance to chase my dreams,
To pursue the passions, that set my soul gleams.
To create, to innovate, to make my mark,
To leave a legacy, amidst the dark.

Give me a chance to love and be loved,
To find a soulmate, with whom I'm beloved.
To share laughter and tears, through thick and thin,
To build a life together, where happiness wins.

Give me a chance to learn and grow,
To expand my horizons, to let knowledge flow.
To embrace wisdom, in all its forms,
To weather life's storms, and weather its norms.

Give me a chance to right my wrongs,
To mend broken bridges, and sing new songs.
To apologize, to forgive, to heal old wounds,
To rebuild trust, under the light of new moons.

Give me a chance to make amends,
To rectify mistakes, and make new friends.
To be a better person, in every way,
To spread kindness and love, day by day.

Give me a chance to find my voice,
To speak my truth, to make my choice.
To stand up for justice, and what is right,
To shine a beacon, in the darkest of night.

Give me a chance to live my best life,
To embrace joy and overcome strife.
To savor each moment, as it comes,
To dance in the rain, and bask in the sun's warmth.

Give me a chance to be myself,
To embrace my quirks, my flaws, my wealth.
To celebrate my uniqueness, with pride,
To walk with confidence, by my side.

Give me a chance to leave my mark,

To make a difference, out in the dark.
To inspire others, to reach for the stars,
To show them that anything is possible, no matter who they are.

So, a chance, give me, to live and to love,
To rise above challenges, with faith from above.
For in every chance, lies a world of possibility,
And with each opportunity, I'll strive for humility.

A chance, give me, to embrace life's dance,
To take the leap, to seize every chance.
For in the end, it's not the chances we take,
But the moments we make, that define our fate.

Two Masters You Can't Serve

Two masters you can't serve, the voice insists,
For in the end, it's yourself you'll resist.
To walk in two directions, is to lose your way,
To be torn apart, in the light of day.

One master demands loyalty, unwavering and true,
To follow its lead, in all that you do.
It's the voice of conscience, the call of the heart,
Guiding your steps, in every part.

The other master is seductive, with promises grand,
But its demands are harsh, its grip like sand.
It whispers sweet nothings, in the ear of the weak,
Leading them astray, with promises bleak.

Two masters you can't serve, for they pull at your soul,
One leads to freedom, the other to control.
One speaks of love, the other of greed,
One plants the seed, the other the weed.

To serve two masters is to betray yourself,
To sacrifice your values, for temporary wealth.
For in the end, it's integrity that stands,
A beacon of light, in the shifting sands.

One master is virtue, the other is sin,
One leads to joy, the other to chagrin.
One fills your heart, with love and grace,
The other leaves emptiness, in its place.

Two masters you can't serve, for they lead to different ends,
One to fulfillment, the other to bends.
One to peace, the other to strife,
One to abundance, the other to life.

So choose your master wisely, with care and thought,
For the path you choose, is the one you'll be caught.
Serve with devotion, with all that you are,
And let your guiding light, be your northern star.

For in the end, it's not the wealth you amass,
But the love in your heart, that will truly last.
So serve your master well, with honor and grace,
And let your journey be a testament, to your inner space.

The Stars Told Me About You

The stars told me about you, in whispers of light,
As they painted the heavens, with shimmering might.
They whispered your name, in the language of stars,
A symphony of beauty, that transcends all bars.

They spoke of your essence, your spirit so pure,
A radiant beacon, that will always endure.
They told of your kindness, your warmth, your grace,
A gentle presence, in the cosmic embrace.

The stars told me about you, in patterns of fire,
As they danced in the heavens, with infinite desire.
They traced your journey, across the night sky,
A celestial ballet, where souls intertwine and fly.

They revealed your secrets, your dreams, your fears,
As they twinkled above, in the darkness clear.
They whispered your hopes, your wishes, your sighs,
A silent prayer, that reaches the skies.

The stars told me about you, in the silence of night,
As they shimmered and sparkled, with radiant light.
They revealed your story, in the tapestry above,
A cosmic connection, built on trust and love.

They showed me your laughter, your tears, your pain,
As they twinkled and danced, in the celestial domain.
They painted your portrait, in shades of stardust,
A masterpiece of beauty, in the infinite crust.

The stars told me about you, in the language of the soul,
As they whispered secrets, that only they know.
They sang of your presence, your spirit so bright,
A guiding light, in the depths of the night.

They whispered your name, in the silence profound,
As they circled above, in the cosmic surround.
They revealed your heart, in the stars' gentle glow,
A timeless connection, that continues to grow.

The stars told me about you, in a symphony divine,
As they painted the heavens, with colors sublime.
They spoke of your essence, your spirit so true,
And in their light, I saw the beauty of you.

So when you gaze upon the stars, in the stillness of night,

Remember the whispers, that shimmer with light.
For in the cosmic dance, where dreams come alive,
The stars told me about you, in a love that will thrive.

Unfortunate Luck

Unfortunate luck, like a shadow cast,
Follows their footsteps, from the present to past.
It colors their days, with shades of gray,
And fills their nights, with silent dismay.

It's the missed opportunities, the doors that close,
The dreams deferred, like wilted rose.
It's the setbacks and challenges, they face each day,
That test their resolve, in every way.

Unfortunate luck, like a heavy cloud,
Hangs over their heads, like a shroud.
It dims their hopes, it dims their light,
And leaves them wandering, in the darkest night.

It's the job they lost, despite their best try,
The love that faded, without a goodbye.
It's the health that wanes, the pain that lingers,
The heart that breaks, with every finger.

Unfortunate luck, like a relentless storm,
Rages on, without reform.
It's the debts that pile, the bills unpaid,
The struggles endured, in the debts' cruel trade.

It's the accidents, the tragedies, the unforeseen,
That turn their lives, to shades of spleen.
It's the losses they bear, the grief they endure,
That leaves their hearts, battered and sore.

Unfortunate luck, like a shadow cast,
Leaves them wondering, how long it will last.
It's the unfairness of life, the cruel twist of fate,
That leaves them feeling, forever second-rate.

But in the midst of darkness, there's a glimmer of light,
A flicker of hope, in the depths of night.
For even in the face of unfortunate luck,
There's strength to be found, in the struggle and muck.

It's the resilience they show, in the face of despair,
The courage to rise, when life isn't fair.
It's the kindness they share, despite their own pain,
The love they give, again and again.

Unfortunate luck may linger, it's true,

But so does the strength, that carries them through.
For in the midst of adversity, they find their power,
And in their darkest hour, they bloom like a flower.

So let us not judge, those with unfortunate luck,
For they carry burdens, that many would shuck.
Let us offer kindness, let us lend a hand,
And help them find hope, in a world unplanned.

For in the tapestry of fate, where threads intertwine,
There's beauty in resilience, there's strength in decline.
And though unfortunate luck may dim their light,
It can never extinguish, their spirit's might.

Dreams Fall Apart

Dreams fall apart, like fragile glass,
Shattering in moments that swiftly pass.
They crumble beneath the weight of fear,
Leaving only echoes we barely hear.

It's the missed opportunity, the door closed tight,
The effort made, but not quite right.
The path once clear, now veiled in mist,
The chance of a lifetime, silently missed.

Dreams fall apart, in the still of night,
When doubts arise, obscuring the light.
They wither like flowers, untouched by sun,
Fading away, one by one.

It's the love that fades, despite our fight,
The cherished plans, that lose their might.
The partnership that failed to thrive,
Leaving us wondering how to survive.

Dreams fall apart, in the relentless tide,
Of time's passage, that will not bide.
The youthful vigor, that wanes with age,
The story left unfinished, on an empty page.

It's the career that falters, the path unclear,
The ambitions thwarted, year after year.
The recognition sought, that never came,
The forgotten name, lost in the game.

Dreams fall apart, in the face of pain,
The hopes washed away, like tears in rain.
The health that fails, the body that weakens,
The spirit crushed, as sorrow deepens.

It's the friendship that drifted, torn by strife,
The bond once cherished, now absent in life.
The trust that shattered, beyond repair,
Leaving a void, too vast to bear.

Dreams fall apart, like autumn leaves,
Scattered by winds, as the heart grieves.
They flutter away, in the chilling breeze,
Leaving behind, memories that tease.

But in the ruins of dreams once bright,

There lies a glimmer, a flicker of light.
For in the broken pieces, we find our strength,
To build anew, to go the length.

When dreams fall apart, we learn to mend,
To reshape our hopes, to find new ends.
We gather the fragments, with tender care,
And weave new dreams, from the despair.

It's in the darkness, we find our flame,
To reignite our passions, to reclaim our name.
We rise from the ashes, with renewed might,
To chase new dreams, in the dawn's light.

For though dreams fall apart, as they often do,
It's in their falling, we find the true.
The courage to dream, again and again,
To face the unknown, to endure the pain.

So let us dream, with hearts unafraid,
For in every ending, new dreams are made.
And though they may fall, and tear us apart,
We'll rise again, with hope in our heart.

I Promised Her

I promised her, in the softest of tones,
A vow made under twilight, where love alone
Could bind our hearts, in a sacred tether,
A commitment to face all storms together.

I promised her a life, not devoid of care,
But one where love and trust would always be there.
To hold her hand through trials and pain,
To stand by her side in sunshine and rain.

I promised her laughter, in moments of glee,
To share in her joys, to set her spirit free.
To dance with her under the moon's gentle light,
To cherish her presence in the quiet of night.

I promised her comfort, in times of distress,
To be her anchor, her source of rest.
To wipe away tears, to soothe her fears,
To be her strength through the years.

I promised her honesty, in all that I do,
To speak my heart, to always be true.
To share my thoughts, my hopes, my dreams,
To build with her a life that gleams.

I promised her patience, when tempers would flare,
To meet her anger with a gentle care.
To listen with empathy, to understand,
To navigate together, hand in hand.

I promised her passion, in every embrace,
To cherish her touch, her tender grace.
To kindle the flames of love anew,
To be her lover, constant and true.

I promised her adventure, in life's grand quest,
To explore new horizons, to seek the best.
To travel together, to places unknown,
To make every moment, a journey home.

I promised her support, in her wildest dreams,
To cheer her on, to be her team.
To believe in her, when doubts arise,
To be the reflection of her bright skies.

I promised her growth, in life's ebb and flow,

To learn and evolve, to let our love grow.
To face the challenges, to embrace the change,
To find new depths, to rearrange.

I promised her forgiveness, for times we might fail,
To mend the rifts, to set sail
On the sea of reconciliation, where love guides the way,
To find new beginnings, each and every day.

I promised her friendship, a bond so deep,
To be her confidant, her secrets to keep.
To laugh together, to share in the fun,
To be her partner, when day is done.

I promised her family, a home of love,
Blessed by the heavens, the stars above.
To build a haven, warm and bright,
A sanctuary of peace, in the darkest night.

I promised her forever, a timeless vow,
To love her always, in the here and now.
To cherish her soul, her heart, her mind,
To be the love she deserves to find.

I promised her these things, with all my heart,
A pledge of devotion, from the very start.

For in her eyes, I found my truth,
A love that transcends, eternal and smooth.

I promised her everything, and so much more,
A love that's boundless, an open door.
For in this promise, we both shall thrive,
A testament to love, that keeps us alive.

I promised her my all, my soul, my being,
A love so pure, it's all-seeing.
And in this promise, we shall find,
A love eternal, deeply intertwined.

Win or Perish

Win or perish, the challenge proclaimed,
To forge ahead, through trials unchained.
To rise above the fray, with courage untamed,
To play the game of life, with glory and fame.

It's the athlete's creed, the warrior's call,
To give their all, to stand tall.
To push beyond the limits, to defy the odds,
To seek the triumph, against all frauds.

Win or perish, in the face of strife,
To grasp the reins of a meaningful life.
To battle despair, to conquer doubt,
To roar with pride, in a victory shout.

It's the student's quest, the scholar's aim,
To master knowledge, to stake their claim.
To delve into wisdom, with fervent zeal,
To illuminate the mind, to forge the steel.

Win or perish, in the pursuit of dreams,
To navigate the torrents, to cross the streams.
To challenge the status quo, to innovate,
To build a legacy, to create our fate.

It's the artist's plight, the poet's muse,
To capture beauty, to refuse to lose.
To paint with passion, to write with fire,
To leave a mark, that will inspire.

Win or perish, in the business world,
To ride the wave, with sails unfurled.
To lead with vision, to strategize,
To turn ambition, into enterprise.

It's the leader's burden, the politician's stake,
To guide with wisdom, for the people's sake.
To craft policies, to enact change,
To heal the wounds, to rearrange.

Win or perish, in the battle of hearts,
To love with abandon, to play our parts.
To cherish the moments, to fight for love,
To nurture the bond, like a mourning dove.

It's the parent's role, the guardian's task,

To raise the future, behind the mask.
To teach with patience, to guide with care,
To build a foundation, that will always be there.

Win or perish, in the face of death,
To seize each day, to draw each breath.
To live with purpose, to embrace the fight,
To seek the truth, to find the light.

It's the human spirit, the will to thrive,
To overcome obstacles, to feel alive.
To face the darkness, with steadfast might,
To claim our victory, in the dead of night.

Win or perish, the creed we hold,
A timeless tale, of the brave and bold.
To rise from ashes, to conquer fate,
To etch our names, on destiny's slate.

For in this life, where battles rage,
We write our story, page by page.
Win or perish, in every breath,
To live with honor, until our death.

So heed the call, with heart and mind,
To win or perish, leave doubt behind.

For in the struggle, we find our strength,
To journey on, to any length.

Win or perish, with spirit anew,
To chase our dreams, to see them through.
For in the end, it's not the win or loss,
But the courage to fight, no matter the cost.

Forty Years

Forty years of suffering, etched in the soul,
The burden heavy, the scars take their toll.
Through the seasons of life, where hope ebbs and flows,
A silent struggle, that nobody knows.

It's the loss of loved ones, taken too soon,
The endless nights, under a mournful moon.
It's the dreams deferred, the goals unmet,
The constant weight of lingering regret.

Forty years of suffering, a relentless tide,
Washing over the spirit, where shadows reside.
Through the corridors of pain, where echoes cry,
A solitary figure walks, asking why.

It's the battles with illness, the body's decay,
The spirit's endurance, in the light of day.
The countless treatments, the never-ending fight,
To grasp at life, with all their might.

Forty years of suffering, in the silence of night,
Where fears are whispered, out of sight.
In the depths of despair, where shadows loom,
A heart still beats, amidst the gloom.

It's the betrayal of friends, the trust betrayed,
The harsh words spoken, the kindness delayed.
It's the isolation felt, in a crowded room,
The smile that's forced, to mask the gloom.

Forty years of suffering, with strength untold,
A life of endurance, a spirit bold.
Through the tears and pain, the constant strife,
A testament to the will to live a life.

It's the dreams that shattered, like fragile glass,
The hopes that faded, as the years pass.
It's the weight of responsibility, the burdens borne,
The silent prayers, in the early morn.

Forty years of suffering, yet still they stand,
A pillar of resilience, in life's shifting sand.
Through the storms of fate, and the winds of woe,
A heart of courage, begins to grow.

It's the lessons learned, through pain and grief,

The moments of respite, however brief.
It's the beauty found, in a simple smile,
The fleeting joy, that makes it worthwhile.

Forty years of suffering, a journey long,
Yet in the darkness, there's still a song.
A melody of hope, that softly plays,
In the quiet moments, it gently sways.

It's the strength of the spirit, that refuses to break,
The will to continue, for love's sake.
It's the bonds of family, the ties that bind,
The love that endures, through the tests of time.

Forty years of suffering, but not in vain,
For through the sorrow, they've learned to gain.
A deeper understanding, a wisdom profound,
A resilience that's forged, from the ground.

It's the quiet victories, the battles won,
The moments of peace, when day is done.
It's the laughter shared, amidst the tears,
The comfort found, in the passing years.

Forty years of suffering, and yet they rise,
A phoenix reborn, beneath the skies.

For in the heart, where pain once reigned,
A flame of hope, has now been gained.

It's the journey of life, with all its scars,
The nights of darkness, beneath the stars.
It's the strength to endure, to find the light,
To face the dawn, after the night.

Forty years of suffering, a testament true,
To the human spirit, that endures anew.
For in the face of pain, and endless night,
There lies the promise, of the coming light.

The Brush is yours

You stand before this empty slate,
With dreams unfurled, you contemplate,
The colors of your heart and mind,
A journey yet to be defined.

With brush in hand and palette wide,
You paint yourself, your soul's true guide,
Through strokes of courage, hues of grace,
A portrait forms, a time, a place.

In dawn's soft glow, your youth unfolds,
With vibrant reds and daring golds,
A spirit wild, a heart unchained,
In every line, your truth is framed.

You paint your laughter, bright and clear,
A burst of yellow, warm and dear,
And shadows too, of doubt and fear,
In shades of blue, your path appears.

Through trials faced and lessons learned,
In emerald greens, your wisdom earned,
You trace the scars, both deep and slight,
With silvered grace, they catch the light.

In love's embrace, you find your muse,
With tender pinks and passionate hues,
A dance of hearts, both lost and found,
In every curve, your hopes abound.

The seasons change, as time flows by,
With autumn's browns and winter's sigh,
You paint the years, both swift and slow,
In every shade, your story grows.

You paint the moments, fleeting, rare,
Of quiet peace, of fervent prayer,
In purples deep and softest white,
A blend of calm and inner light.

Through failures faced and triumphs claimed,
You paint the dreams you've yet to name,
In every layer, thick or thin,
A deeper truth begins to spin.

For in this act of self-creation,

You find a form of liberation,
A canvas wide, where you define,
The essence of your inner line.

In every brushstroke, bold or shy,
You paint your tears, your laughter, sigh,
A testament to who you are,
A journey marked by every scar.

The world may see a finished frame,
Yet never know from whence it came,
For only you can truly tell,
The stories that your strokes compel.

In moments dark, when colors fade,
When doubts arise and dreams cascade,
Remember this: the brush is yours,
To paint anew, to open doors.

For life itself is art, untamed,
A masterpiece that can't be named,
By one alone, but by each breath,
You paint your path, from birth to death.

So paint yourself, with joy and pain,
With sunshine bright and gentle rain,

With every hue that life bestows,
In every stroke, your spirit grows.

You are the artist of your fate,
With every choice, a stroke you make,
So let your colors dance and play,
And paint yourself, in your own way.

So here you stand, with brush in hand,
A soul that seeks to understand,
The beauty in each fleeting day,
You paint yourself, come what may.

Sign Up for Success

Sign up for success, it calls, with a voice both bold and clear,
Embrace the path before you, dispel each doubt and fear.
For in the heart of striving, where dreams and action meet,
Lies the seed of greatness, in every goal you greet.

The journey starts within you, with a vision in your mind,
A spark of inspiration, a purpose well-defined.
Success is not a moment, it's a road of twists and turns,
A marathon of effort, where every failure burns.

Each setback is a lesson, each stumble a new start,
The fire of determination ignites within your heart.
Sign up for success, it whispers, take courage in your stride,
For in the face of challenges, let confidence be your guide.

The world is full of voices, of naysayers and doubt,
But your inner voice of reason will lead you on the route.
To climb the tallest mountains, to sail uncharted seas,
To build a life of meaning, fulfilling destinies.

Success is in the choices, the habits that you form,
In the discipline of morning, in the calm amidst the storm.
It's waking up with purpose, it's sleeping with a plan,
It's knowing when to persevere, and when to take a stand.

Sign up for success, it calls, in moments grand and small,
In the way you face each challenge, in how you rise from every fall.
It's not about perfection, but progress day by day,
It's the wisdom in persistence, in finding your own way.

In the quiet of the evening, when the world has gone to rest,
Reflect upon your journey, on how you've given your best.
Success is in the striving, in the courage to pursue,
In the heart that never wavers, in the spirit that is true.

Sign up for success, it beckons, in the dawn's first gentle light,
In the tasks that lie before you, in the dreams that take to flight.
It's in the books you study, the wisdom that you glean,
In the way you shape your future, from visions you have seen.

Success is in the giving, in the love you freely share,
In the way you lift up others, in the times you truly care.
It's in the joy of service, in the work that lights your soul,
In the art of finding balance, in making yourself whole.

Sign up for success, it calls, a banner to unfurl,

In the journey of becoming, in shaping your own world.
For success is not a destination, but a life lived with intent,
A legacy of purpose, a life well spent.

So heed the call of promise, of potential in your hand,
Sign up for success today, take a bold and fearless stand.
For in the heart of striving, in the courage to be true,
Lies the path to greatness, and the best of you.

Embrace each day's new challenges, let your passions be your guide,
With resilience as your compass, and ambition by your side.
For the road to success is winding, with trials yet unseen,
But with a heart committed, you'll achieve what others deem.

Sign up for success, it whispers, a journey to embark,
With every step you take, you'll leave an indelible mark.
In the annals of your history, in the echoes of your name,
You'll find that true success is more than fortune or acclaim.

It's in the quiet victories, in the battles hard and won,
In the story of your journey, in the rising of the sun.
Sign up for success, embrace it, with a spirit strong and free,
For the path to your own greatness begins with just one plea.

Be the Candle

Be the candle, small yet bright, a beacon in the night,
For in your flame there's courage, a soft and guiding light.
You may not banish shadows, nor end the dark's domain,
But in your steadfast glowing, you'll soothe the heart's refrain.

In the halls of deep despair, where sorrow casts its shade,
Where hope seems but a memory, and joy begins to fade,
Be the candle, ever glowing, a symbol of the dawn,
For even in the bleakest night, the smallest light lives on.

The world is full of turmoil, of chaos and of pain,
A symphony of suffering, a never-ending strain.
Yet in the midst of all this, where chaos seeks to reign,
Be the candle, softly burning, to ease another's pain.

In every act of kindness, in every gentle word,
In every smile that brightens, a weary soul unheard,
Be the candle, bringing warmth, where coldness grips the heart,
For in your light, there blossoms, a chance for a new start.

Life's burdens may be heavy, the path ahead unclear,
But in your inner brightness, there lies a way to steer.
Be the candle, steadfast, true, unwavering in the gale,
For in your glow of resilience, no storm can make you pale.

The world may often challenge, may seek to snuff your flame,
With trials and tribulations, with struggles just the same.
But in your core, remember, the light that you possess,
Be the candle, undiminished, in moments of duress.

In every darkened corner, where shadows deeply cling,
In every place of mourning, where silent tears do spring,
Be the candle, softly shining, a promise of the day,
For in your light, a whisper, of a brighter, kinder way.

When dreams are all but shattered, and hopes lie in dismay,
When love seems but a memory, and joy has gone astray,
Be the candle, softly burning, a symbol of the fight,
For in your flame of passion, lies the power of the light.

The world is vast and varied, with mountains high and low,
With valleys filled with shadows, where cold winds often blow.
Yet in each heart, there lingers, a spark of purest gold,
Be the candle, gently glowing, in stories yet untold.

Through trials and through triumphs, through laughter and through
tears,
Be the candle, ever present, throughout the passing years.
For in your light, there's wisdom, in your flame, a guide,
Be the candle, softly glowing, through life's uncertain ride.

When the night seems never-ending, and dawn feels far away,
When courage starts to falter, and strength begins to sway,
Be the candle, steadfast, true, a constant in the dark,
For in your light, there's power, to ignite a hopeful spark.

In the quiet of the morning, in the stillness of the night,
In the moments in between, where dreams take flight,
Be the candle, gently glowing, a beacon in the storm,
For in your light, there's healing, a place of being warm.

Be the candle, in your heart, let your light be seen,
In the kindness you extend, in the places you have been.
For in this world of darkness, of shadows deep and wide,
Be the candle, softly glowing, with love as your guide.

So let your flame keep burning, through every storm and trial,
Be the candle in the darkness, with a heart that will not wile.
For in your light, there's meaning, a purpose pure and true,
Be the candle, ever glowing, with a light that's born anew.

Be the candle, shining bright, a beacon in the night,
For in your light, there's hope, a future shining bright.
Be the candle, softly glowing, through every trial and fight,
For in your flame, there's power, to bring the world to light.

www.ingramcontent.com/pod-product-compliance
Lightning Source LLC
Chambersburg PA
CBHW060929140726
47996CB00001B/431